The Way To Self-Development

THE WAY TO SELF-DEVELOPMENT

GEORGE KIOURTZIDIS

Copyright © 2019 George Kiourtzidis

The moral right of the author has been asserted.

Apart from any fair dealing for the purposes of research or private study, or criticism or review, as permitted under the Copyright, Designs and Patents Act 1988, this publication may only be reproduced, stored or transmitted, in any form or by any means, with the prior permission in writing of the publishers, or in the case of reprographic reproduction in accordance with the terms of licences issued by the Copyright Licensing Agency. Enquiries concerning reproduction outside those terms should be sent to the publishers.

The manufacturer's authorised representative in the EU for product safety is Authorised Rep Compliance Ltd, 71 Lower Baggot Street, Dublin D02 P593 Ireland (www.arccompliance.com)

Matador
9 Priory Business Park,
Wistow Road, Kibworth Beauchamp,
Leicestershire. LE8 0RX
Tel: 0116 279 2299
Email: books@troubador.co.uk
Web: www.troubador.co.uk/matador
Twitter: @matadorbooks

ISBN 978 178901 499 0

British Library Cataloguing in Publication Data.
A catalogue record for this book is available from the British Library.

Printed by 4Edge Ltd
Typeset in 11pt Minion Pro by Troubador Publishing Ltd, Leicester, UK

Matador is an imprint of Troubador Publishing Ltd

CONTENTS

	PREFACE	ix
1.	INTRODUCTION	1
2.	CONSCIENCE, PERSONALITY AND THE LAW OF THREE	5
3.	THE METHOD	15
4.	LOVE YOUR NEIGHBOUR	27
5.	ESOTERIC CHRISTIANITY	39
6.	ESOTERIC MEANING OF THE GOSPELS	45
7.	MYTHS, LEGENDS AND MESSENGERS	67
8.	MY STORY	75
9.	THE OBSERVED AND THE OBSERVER	83

PREFACE

This book is the result of my life events combined with the work of my grandfather's first cousin G.I. Gurdjieff and the wisdom that has been handed to us through the ages. It serves as a practical guide to self-development. My aim is to reveal the knowledge of truth in practice, without writing in double meaning as in the gospels, parables, myths and other allegories.

George Kiourtzidis
all-and-everything.org

1

INTRODUCTION

Once upon a time, thousands of years ago, there was a civilisation, the Babylonian civilisation, in which everyone spoke a common language. And at a certain point, the people took the decision to build a tower to reach the skies. But instead of using stones, they built it with bricks, and used slime for mortar. For that reason, the tower fell and they were dispersed like sheep without a shepherd.

Stones in such ancient scriptures signify knowledge of God-made laws (the Ten Commandments were written on stones). To reach the skies, to reach a higher level, we first need the knowledge of truth and then build on it, by doing what we know is true. Only by doing what we know is true, by living according to our conscience, will we understand. And when that happens, we will agree with each other, we will all speak a common language, because conscience is the same to everyone. But as soon as our education starts, which is conducted under man-made laws as in the bricks, we begin to take everything we read and hear literally.

Knowledge alone is fragmented, contradictory and will always lead to destruction. Those with knowledge alone may speak about the same things as the person with understanding, but their speech is fragmented; they talk about different things at different times. They are what they talk about; one moment this, another moment that. There is no connection to what they might say next, no unity. They think they understand because they have knowledge, but knowledge alone does not make the whole of a person. Knowledge without understanding is contradictory.

Understanding cancels all contradictions. Understanding is the unification of everything. Only a person who is all things at all times has understanding, which comes from the conscience, not from the *evidence of the senses* (what we see and hear) alone. When we understand the knowledge of truth, we talk from within; though we speak about the knowledge of truth, everything that we say or do comes from us. Everything is connected; we are the truth.

Such a person is a whole, unique human being, not an imitation of other people. Imitation, the desire to 'do as others do', is represented by using slime for mortar in the Tower of Babel story.

The meaning of the story is no truer than today. Modern civilisation has given us material comfort and is constantly reaching new boundaries in science, technology and medicine. But it has taken away the essential qualities that we need for our harmonious development. With all the influences that we are now under – television, fashion and all the technology around us – we are more than ever a stranger to that inner life that should be ours by right. As C.S. Nott writes:

> *'The life of our time has become so complex that man has deviated from his original type.'*
> *(C.S. Nott, 'Teachings of Gurdjieff' 1961)*

Self-development – How and Why

Messengers such as Christ, Buddha, and others have given us the knowledge we need for our development. However, as we will see, much of this knowledge cannot be taken literally to be properly understood. Therefore, we do not find much practical guidance on *how* we should apply it in our daily lives, and especially *why*. And that is the aim of this book, to give the *how* and *why*. It provides a practical method to free us from those external influences that prevent us from living a natural life, allowing us to instead be ourselves, our real selves, not simply imitations of others. Only then will we gain understanding of the knowledge that has been handed down to us.

Without understanding, there will always be ego and vanity, as in the New Testament gospels when Jesus overturned the tables of the moneylenders in the temple, and of those that were selling doves. Knowledge alone always fell into the hands of the moneylenders, those who were doing the teaching for their own self-interest. And those who were selling doves (the purest of all animals) were selling their hearts, the purest place in us, out of vanity.

Vanity will make us sacrifice almost everything to protect a certain entity. And that entity is none other than our 'false' self, which will sacrifice friendships, even a family member, in order not to be proven wrong.

This book is about the development of our real self. It will show you where to begin the journey and which method to use, so that all knowledge of truth and good will become your property. It is for everyone and anyone, regardless of their background, culture or upbringing.

2

CONSCIENCE, PERSONALITY AND THE LAW OF THREE

To understand our present condition, let us speak about conscience, personality and the three centres. Later in this book, I will give examples of these levels of being in esoteric Christianity and other scriptural and mythological allegories.

Conscience and Personality

He that loveth father or mother more than me is not worthy of me.

(Matthew 10:34-37)

He who loves his mother or father more than his conscience is not worthy of his conscience. Conscience in us is our own. Personality in us is not our own but that which comes from the outside, what we have learned and stored in our memory, all words and movements that we have acquired, all feelings created by imitation.

A small child has no personality yet. The child is what he or she really is: its *essence*. But by living among people who indulge their negative emotions, the child automatically acquires them. Personality is created by the influences of other people – that is, by education, by imitation, by our culture. Education creates personality. The whole of our life, all that we call civilisation and politics, is created by people's personality – that is, by what is not their own.

Personality is formed from the mind. We are not our minds; we are what we do. When we live by our mind alone, we live according to our 'false personality'. We act and react in life as people always do, in the same old ways, because the mind is always repeating the same things over and over. We become identified with our minds. Let's make the connection with the following parable:

> *The kingdom of heaven is likened unto a man that sowed good seed in his field, but while men slept, his enemy came and sowed tares[1] also among the wheat, and went away. But when the blade sprang up, and brought forth fruit, then appeared the tares also. And the servants of the householder came and said to him, "Sir didst thou not sow good seed in thy field? Whence then hath it tares?" And he said unto them, "An enemy hath done this." And the servants say unto him, "Wilt thou then that we go and gather them up?" But he saith, "Nay; lest haply while ye gather up the tares, ye root up the wheat with them. Let both grow together until the harvest, and in the time of the harvest I will say to the reapers, Gather up first the tares and bind them in bundles to burn them, but gather the wheat into my barn." (Matthew 13:24–30)*

---

1   weeds

The good seed represents the real side of us. The field is our essence. But when the man slept, when there was no *attention*, the weeds appeared (I will speak about attention in the next chapter). The weeds in humankind are our false personality. We need to get rid of them, bind them in bundles and burn them as in the parable, or as I like to say 'let them rot', so that we can change our level of being. False personality, formed by our upbringing and through the influences from our surroundings, which muddle and disfigure the real side of us, is the primary cause of all misunderstandings arising in everyday life.

Peaceful human existence and happiness depend almost entirely on the absence of false personality. False personality gives rise to the emotions of ego and self-pride, the means of being easily offended.

Personality, as we have said, is acquired and takes over us at every moment. We live our lives through the lens of our personality, not directly. We do not see our personality, we are not conscious of it, and so we don't feel present. Instead, we feel dissatisfied with life and so we blame others and try to find fault in them. We are not sincere.

And so we are always carrying our personality about with us, and always hoping, perhaps, that if only we had a new environment, if only we were to go on a holiday and, let's say, meet new people, then everything would be completely different. How could that be, since we are always carrying our Sinbad's bag about with us – our personality – with all its manners acquired through imitation. Manners of walking, manners of speaking, finding fault in others, and so on. We are influenced by almost everything we can see around us, especially fashions, television, the media and modern technology.

The Three Centres

In our civilisation, over the centuries, our inner world has become so complex, and still this carries on. One of the reasons is that after the age of twenty or so, people stop thinking originally. They think mechanically, repetitively, and this lies in the failure to get in touch with our conscience. By getting in touch with our conscience, the real side of us, we develop our objective reasoning, which is under the Law of Three – the three centres of our being acting simultaneously together.

When we develop ourselves and live according to our conscience, we never repeat. We become spontaneous, we are all things at all times, our life is in abundance, we live in Eternity.

Let's put down the three centres of a person:

> The Intellectual Centre;
>
> The Emotional Centre;

and The Instinctive Moving Centre.

The Intellectual Centre, associated with the mind, makes us capable of logic and reasoning. The mind is a form of storage. It takes in what we put in – all knowledge from life; everything from our senses; from education; all words, good or bad; all knowledge, true or false, right or wrong.

The Emotional Centre makes us capable of feeling. The way we are in touch with our bodies today means our Emotional Centre is either too dominant or lacking. A person whose Emotional Centre is lacking is often under the influences of vanity and self-conceit; such a person is not sincere. On the other hand, those whose Emotional Centre is too dominant are unable to control their negative reactions.

And as for the Moving Centre, this faculty controls the muscles of the body. When the muscles are relaxed, we are in control of the body. But when the negative part of the Emotional Centre is involved, the Moving Centre weakens, and thus follows uncontrolled physical manifestations, like tension.

Balancing the Centres

In a normal way of life, the Emotional and Instinctive Moving Centres should develop naturally, since the Intellectual Centre is already present. All three centres in a person must work together, and simultaneously, with none of them stronger than the others. And when we arrive at that point, we stop thinking mechanically. Thinking mechanically involves only one or two centres. And since we use only one or two of our centres, we do not possess objective reason. When only one or two centres are involved, false personality arises, which is very difficult to redress.

The difficulty comes down to the fact that we have no accurate knowledge of how our bodies work. I have a body, and I wish to learn how to use it. I wish for no one from outside to conquer my body, not even false personality. And this has been given to us through the ages. Many myths, including Atlantis, Pandora's Box, Hercules and St George, can be interpreted as freeing ourselves from false personality.

But knowledge alone is not enough. There is a method that I will make clear, a method that provides a technique for using the three centres of our body for our own aim, our development, since we are created as self-developing organisms.

The *What* to do comes from the Intellectual Centre; *How* is from the Moving Centre, and *Why* comes from the Emotional Centre. The mind knows, the conscience perceives, the body feels and the heart speaks or does.

If your Emotional Centre is always present but too dominant, there is a need to work on the Moving Centre and bring the Emotional Centre down to the level where it should be. For that to happen, I will provide a method for relaxing the muscles, lowering the shoulders and loosening the wrists. And by being in such a state, you will have control over your body. There will be no more tension, you will have the power, and your Intellectual and Moving Centres will together bring the Emotional Centre down to their level, so that all three centres become equal, with none stronger than the others. They form a triad and act simultaneously and harmoniously.

And since this book is about self-development, I will speak about the Law of Three that we are under, according to our nature, and the three forces that must take part every day, every minute of the day, for our development. That is why it has been said that man, with his own efforts, can become the image of God. God is under the Law of Three.

The Three Forces

I will now describe the three forces, the knowledge that has been passed down to us, that God is in Trinity, and Trinity is in Unity. Namely:

The Holy Affirming;

The Holy Denying;

The Holy Reconciling.

And since we have been created in the image of God, we are also under the Law of Three. For anything real to happen in any event, three forces must be present. And in a human, they are:

Active or positive;

Denying or negative;

Neutralising or Reconciling.

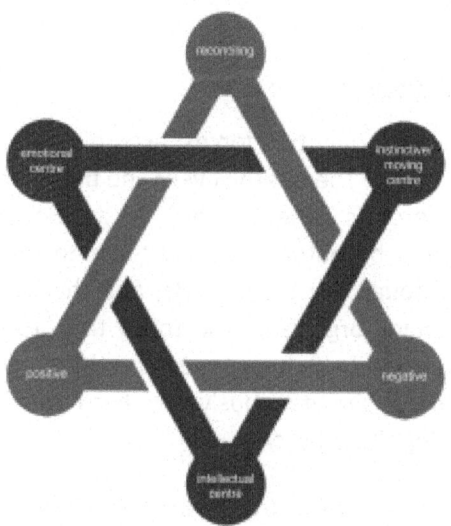

Figure 1: The three centres and the three forces.

By not reacting negatively to unpleasant events, we create the reconciling force; there is a unity in us.

And that is the aim of the Greek philosopher Socrates in the following account. Socrates had all the necessary knowledge, but he had to do what he knew was true. And for that, he went and married Xanthippe. Xanthippe was known to be the most argumentative woman in Athens, so by not reacting to disagreeable events, Socrates would bring about in himself the reconciling force.

When asked by one of his pupils why he chose to live with such a wife he answered, "Mankind at large is what I wish to deal and associate with; and so I have got her, well assured that if I can endure her, I shall have no difficulty in my relations with all the rest of mankind."

The Reconciling Force

Today we live under only two forces, according to our nature – positive and negative. There is the event and there is the reaction, but the third force is absent. Why? Because the reconciling force is not given by nature. We must create the third force by ourselves, through our own efforts, and that is what makes us a self-developing organism. And to do that, to develop the reconciling force, we have been given the three centres, as we said earlier, to use simultaneously and harmoniously, without one overpowering the others.

When only two forces take part, the positive and the negative, or the event and the reaction, then follows the result of the process – the reciprocal destruction of the two opposite forces, as shown in Gurdjieff's analogy:

> *'...if you imagine yourself high up and looking down upon a large public square, where thousands, seized with the most intense form of their chief psychosis, are destroying each other's existence by all kinds of means invented by them themselves, and that in their places there immediately appear what are called their*

> *'corpses', which owing to the outrages done to them by the beings who are not yet destroyed, change colour very perceptibly, as a result of which the general visibility of the surface of the said large square is gradually changed* (changed with their own blood and corpses everywhere)'
>
> *(Beelzebub's Tales to His Grandson, G.I. Gurdjieff)*

And still this carries on. But we have the capability, by making the necessary effort, by insisting and persisting, by not giving up, until we create the third force – the reconciling force – so that our inner world can be transformed into gold. Real gold, which all the gold on Earth cannot buy.

The union of the three forces and the three centres acting simultaneously is represented in this verse from the New Testament:

> *And after six days, Jesus taketh with him Peter, and James, and John his brother, and he bringeth them up into a high mountain apart: and he was transfigured before them; and his face did shine as the sun, and his garments became white as the light.*
>
> *(Matthew. 17:1–2)*

Six days in the gospels signifies the completion of a person. When we do what we know is true, then we understand. And that happens when all of our three centres – the Intellectual, Emotional and Moving centres – work together and simultaneously. And when that takes place, then follows another completion, the union of the three forces – the positive, negative and reconciling forces.

And the outcome of the moment when all three centres and forces are at play is a transfiguration ('he was transfigured before them'), which is the meaning of when Jesus became Christ. The change was one hundred percent, and so it is when we speak and do from the heart. When we speak from the heart, there is no tension in the face ('and his face did shine as the sun'). When we speak or act from the heart, we turn the knowledge of truth into good and there is light in the heart ('and his garments became white as the light').

3

THE METHOD

Around 33 years ago, I was obliged to discover a method for curing my physical and spiritual bodies, which no man-made medicine could do for me. This path of self-development involves three interconnected parts and is represented in the diagram on the following page.

- Breathing
- Attention
- Self-observation

The air that we breathe forms an electric wire, let's say, linking all the parts of our development. This 'wire' is represented by the lines in the diagram. We can connect this with the first of the two commandments given by Jesus in the New Testament:

> *Thou shalt love the Lord thy God with all thy heart, and with all thy soul, and with all thy mind, and with all thy strength.*
>
> *(Mark 12:30)*

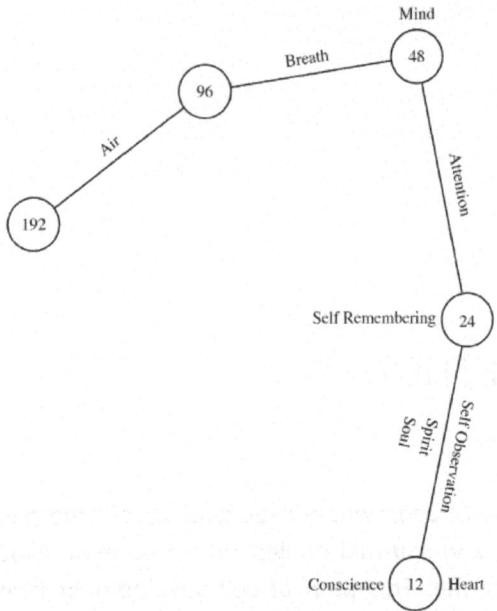

Figure 2: The path of self-development adapted from Gurdjieff's 'Scale of Hydrogens'.

'With all thy heart' – conscience in the heart at point 12.

'With all thy soul' – through self-observation, which creates the soul.

'With all thy strength' – through attention and self-remembering.

'With all thy mind' – at point 48.

Breathing

Let's start at point 96. The air from point 192 goes automatically and naturally to point 96, representing a process that is the same for all living things: breathing.

Breathing plays a vital role in the Method and in our development. Today, we do not breathe properly, and there follows tension, stress and numerous diseases, especially the flu. When we catch the flu frequently, this is a clear sign that we are not breathing properly. When our breathing is regulated, the infection will be kept at bay – except in children, because their bodies are not yet strong enough, and also occasionally while travelling in aeroplanes, because the parts of air that must be exhaled are recirculated in that confined space. I recall in my early age I used to catch the flu two or three times a year, but after doing physical work to regulate my breathing, I never caught it again for thirty years, except once while travelling in an aeroplane.

The reason we do not breathe properly is that from an early age we cease to be in touch with our conscience and therefore do not *remember ourselves* (see Self-observation). And that is why we must do physical work to regulate our breathing and gain attention. In the chapter 'My Story', I describe in detail the voluntary labour that I undertook for this aim.

Remembering ourselves through the air means to get in touch with our conscience: we are our conscience. By regulating the breathing according to this method, the air from point 96, through our breath, is taken in and allows us to use the faculties of the mind which for the moment are not fully active. That is why we are a self-developing organism, so that by our own efforts we can reach the parts of ourselves that are currently undeveloped. That is the starting point. And by doing this, we get in touch with our Intellectual Centre, our mind, at point 48.

At this moment, something happens within us – we get a shock. This shock is nothing other than our attention. It is quite shocking to suddenly have attention and remember oneself, one's real self.

As for a clear and practical proof of why only through our breath do we feel present and have attention, I ask this. How many times has this happened to you? You are walking along a pavement with your mind on everyday events, and suddenly you decide to cross the street, with cars going right and left. As soon as you put one foot out on the street, you are suddenly aware of your present surroundings. You see the danger and stop. And now think: how did you 'remember yourself' at that particular moment? It was your automatic reaction to the dangerous situation; your mind, pointing out the danger of crossing the street, forced you to be present and your reaction was there in a sudden intake and exhalation of air: 'A-AH!' In other words, at that precise moment, your brain, through your breath, told you to pay attention and remember yourself.

So from now on, in anything you do, anything you say, put your mind on your breath first, and then speak or act. By doing this, you have attention, you are present, you remember yourself. And since I am because I breathe, consciousness follows.

Attention and self-observation

Attention is the gap between the Intellectual Centre and self-remembering, as in the diagram, so that we can remember ourselves. By paying attention, you get in touch with your conscience. Keep your attention on your breath and then, and only then, speak or act. By doing this, you will also learn to talk passively, from the heart, through your breath.

A person with attention sees in front, behind, to his left and to his right, all at the same time. How? Only if you put half of your attention on what is happening, and the other half on your breath.

The gap in the diagram between point 24, self-remembering, and point 12, our conscience, is self-observation. To observe ourselves, we must first know what to observe, and that is our minds. We are not our minds; we are what we choose and take out of our minds. There are many things that enter our minds from life's many events – good and bad, right or wrong.

But to observe oneself means to split oneself into two parts. The self that I am now, and the self that observes all my actions. By having attention and remembering ourselves, the second shock appears. As Socrates said: 'I know that I do not know', and this happens when one observes oneself. It is quite shocking to suddenly know that you don't know. And the way out of it is our conscience; only our conscience can perceive what is true and good, not our minds.

The way is this: first, think from the mind what it is you want to say or do, then stop. Then, according to this method, 'bring down' what is in your mind to your conscience through your breath. By putting attention on your breath, the air goes much deeper. Get in touch with your conscience and *think again* from there. Then, and only then, speak or act, if you wish to be correct. Only with the help of our conscience can we find the right way to speak or act. At this point, our development is in motion. We think and act in a new way; we create new experiences that we have never had before. We begin to realise our existence, and we are no longer driven by circumstances.

> *Jesus...was led by the Spirit in the wilderness during forty days, being tempted of the devil. And he did eat nothing in those days: and when they were completed, he hungered.*
>
> *(Luke 4:1–2)*

When we observe ourselves sincerely, we get in touch with our conscience. Sincerity comes from conscience. Then follows the duty of silence, just as Jesus fulfilled in the above verse, signified by his time alone in the wilderness. When we know that we don't know, we become silent and take our time until we are ready.

I recall a conversation with some acquaintances of mine thirty years ago during my visit to the Greek island of Skiathos (which I will mention again in Chapter 8 My Story). At a certain moment, one of them asked me a question which I was not yet ready to answer the right way. So instead I became silent. Although I do not remember the question now, I clearly recall one of these acquaintances saying to me, "Come on George, say it, say it!" But I kept my peace because my conscience wouldn't let me do otherwise.

When we observe ourselves sincerely, the Spirit is formed, which leads to our conscience. We see all the bad influences that affect us. We are in the wilderness, just as Jesus was for forty days. Living according to our conscience, the results are not immediate, since conscience is new territory for us. And we get 'tempted by the Devil' (when we are on the verge of giving up), so a great effort is needed.

When we are 'completed', when we start living according to our conscience, we will hunger for the good of the truth, since conscience is based on what is true and good. Conscience perceives, conscience is spontaneous, in abundance. There is new life at every moment.

Conscience

By now we are at point 12 on the diagram. The air through our breath is the final stage of our self-development. We get in touch with our conscience, we see the kingdom of God, as in the following quote from the Gospels:

> *Unless a man is born from above, he cannot see the kingdom of God.*
>
> *(John 3:3)*

We must first be born from above – this is the way to see the kingdom of God, from above, from the air that we breathe, to make us see that which we already possess in us, our conscience.

Conscience is based on God-made laws, on what is true and good. And since our conscience is in our hearts, we enter our hearts. We enter the kingdom of heaven. By uncovering our buried conscience from above through the air that we breathe, and since it is new territory for us to live according to what is true and good, there must be a rebirth. We can therefore say: unless we are born again, we cannot enter into the kingdom of heaven. And we say born again because we are born with our conscience, but then we lose it.

The rebirth is difficult and slow at first, but neither faint nor fear. Start living according to your conscience, and as time goes by you will get better and better, and there are fountains along the way. By finding the correct answers, the correct way, by living according to our conscience, we see the benefits, we get refreshed.

By getting in touch with our conscience every day, every minute of the day, through the air that we breathe, the answers will come faster and faster, and there will be a time when our conscience will become greater and act faster than our minds.

But there are events in life that may seem difficult to redress, and which prevent us from continuing our development. These events come under two types. While the first are impossible to redress, we can look at the second as intentionally introduced 'from above' for our self-development.

As for the first, when something unforeseen happens, some misfortune or accident, this thing happens for reasons of its own. It is impossible for us to comprehend, and since God is all loving, He created our mind in such a way, to be able to cope with such events.

And the solution in such an event is this: do not become immersed in despondency, since we can do nothing about it. Instead, acknowledge the event and remove it from your mind. But how can this be done? By putting our minds into something else, something of a different order. And this is possible because the mind, by virtue of our creation, can take in only one thing at a time, one thing at any given moment. Try entering two things at once into your mind and you will see it is impossible. What we put in our minds is all down to us.

And now the second kind, which we face almost every day. These events may seem bad at first and are not what we desired. For these, we must always remember the phrase 'every stick always has two ends', and in our situation, one bad and one good end.

THE METHOD

And since God is all loving, He gives us the bad end first, and leaves it to us to try and find the good end of the stick, the good end of the event, using our own reasoning. In everything bad, there is always good. It is down to us to make the effort to find the good end. But we have stopped making the effort, and for that we blame God.

Without those events that seem bad at first, we wouldn't be three-centred beings. We wouldn't have an Intellectual Centre, and we wouldn't be human beings. These events are intentionally introduced from above for us to develop ourselves. And the purpose of this development is to obtain objective reason, since this is the reason for our existence on Earth.

By always asking ourselves why an unexpected, undesirable event has occurred, and by putting two and two together, by using our reasoning, we find the good end, which is always there. And when that happens, we will feel happy. This is real happiness, and it applies to the smallest and the largest events in life. So, make this a way of life. Try to always find the good end of the stick, the good end of the event, and you will see the difference. By making the effort, we have the possibility and the ability to turn the curse into a blessing. That is why it has been said:

> *Ask, and it shall be given you; seek, and ye shall find; knock, and it shall be opened unto you.*
>
> *(Matthew 7:7)*

First we must know *how* to ask, which is that we ask sincerely through our conscience. Sincerity comes from conscience. Conscience is devoid of ego, self-love, self-esteem, self-pride, self-interest, and so on. If we ask sincerely, we will receive. But if by any chance we ask sincerely and things do not happen as we wish, do not despair; it is because we are not yet ready to receive. In time, we will be. When we live according to our conscience, we can never be wrong. Even if things look bad at first, later developments will prove us right. As we said, the mind takes in many things from life's events, but I, not the mind, must choose. However, we must know who 'I' is, and how to choose.

And now let me ask you: what do you want to choose – what is 'good' for you, or what is impartially correct? And since it must be the second, we need to find that place in us that is impartial so we can make the correct decisions.

By applying this method, we will bring together all the functions of our machine, our body, and get in touch with our real side. And by being in touch with our real side, according to this method, every minute of the day, we will develop ourselves by ourselves.

Knock, and it shall be opened unto you.

By insisting and persisting, by not giving up, we become a unity. Our inner world changes, our outer perception changes, our life becomes more vivid. We will be in abundance, in eternity, and the change will be one hundred per cent. Live according to your conscience and you will remain forever young. And since that is and always will be the case, if anyone were to come, including the Devil, and promise us all the gold in the world to go back and be as we were before, we would say, 'No, thank you'.

So, from now on, let this little book be your companion. Follow your conscience and you will receive your reward, a reward that all the gold in the world cannot buy. And for clarity I quote the following verse from the Christian New Testament:

And the devil, taking him up into an high mountain, shewed unto him all the kingdoms of the world in a moment of time. And the devil said unto him, All this power will I give thee, and the glory of them: for that is delivered unto me; and to whomsoever I will I give it. If thou therefore wilt worship me, all shall be thine. And Jesus answered and said unto him, Get thee behind me, Satan: for it is written, Thou shalt worship the Lord thy God, and him only shalt thou serve.

(Luke 4:5–7)

Worship and serve only your conscience. But for this to happen, we must understand and do in practice what is to follow.

4

LOVE YOUR NEIGHBOUR

In Mark 12:28–34, when asked "Which is the greatest commandment in the law?", Jesus answered, "Thou shalt love the Lord thy God with all thy heart, and with all thy soul, and with all thy mind, and with all thy strength", before giving the second commandment, "Thou shalt love thy neighbour as thyself."

The first commandment is about attention and self-remembering, which is represented in Figure 2 (Chapter 3). But it is this second commandment that I will talk about, because therein lies all the misunderstandings of mankind today.

When we say 'Love your neighbour', we must understand who our neighbour is, whether next door, in the next street, the next town, in the desert or another country. We must also understand what 'love' is and what kind of love the saying refers to. The kind of love we are speaking about is conscious love.

Today, no matter what has been said against us, we wish to love our neighbour. But with so many unpleasant events around us and our reaction to them, we find this impossible to do, impossible to comprehend. We need to know HOW to do it, how to show love in practice, and also a reason for doing so, a reason that will unite life's events and our reactions to them. In other words, we need to know WHY we should love our neighbour. The 'why' will be, and should be, to our benefit.

I will now give a few examples of how to love your fellow human being.

Put your neighbour first

In anything you say or do, *put your neighbour first*, which means you consider your neighbour's position first, and "I" must come second. By putting our neighbour first, we understand others, we see our neighbour's perspective, we become intelligent and feel joy. Do that which is good and you will feel the same. And it follows that he who is second shall then become first. I am good to others for me, so I feel the joy of my good actions. And now the Commandment becomes clear: Love your neighbour the way you *should* love yourself.

As we are today, there is one place in our lives where we feel joy, and that is in the family, where we put our children first. And now let us be mothers and fathers of the world, no matter our age.

Put yourself first and you become clever but at the same time stupid. Put your neighbour first and you become intelligent and feel joy.

Be indifferent to personality

Conscious love is indifferent to likes and dislikes. In other words, it should make no difference to me what the other person is like; what counts is who I am, and I am good to everyone.

And this can be done by not taking our senses seriously, since arguing based on the evidence from the senses is useless. We must therefore deceive the senses. By not taking our senses seriously, in other words by not taking what we see and hear seriously, we see very clearly that whenever we get identified with life's events, whenever we become negative with another person, it is always our fault. Do not take yourself seriously and you will see a smile on your face. We are not our senses, we are what we do.

Religious writings contain references to dogs, including passages that appear to refrain people from keeping dogs in the house. I would like to give this a twofold allegorical meaning. The dog is an animal in which we can very clearly see two opposing forces at work – the event and the reaction. Dogs react automatically. So, in the home, if any family member happens to do something disagreeable, do not react as dogs do. Instead, acknowledge it and remove it from your mind, which we achieve by not taking our senses seriously. If we see something wrong, if we hear something unpleasant and we don't take ourselves seriously, no harm is done. We see that it was only a mistake because we didn't know any better. After all, it is rarely intentional in a family. Only by taking ourselves seriously and answering directly does it become intentional.

And as for the second meaning, it is the same with our neighbour. Do not keep dogs in your house. Do not react in your heart.

'Do alms in secret'

As we have said, when you put your neighbour first, "I" must come second. However, when you do good, and then go and speak about it, "I" comes first. You have already received your reward, and that reward is worthless. But when you do good without speaking about it, therefore in secret, you put your neighbour first.

And in this way, you get in touch with your conscience, and since conscience is based on what is true and good, since conscience is in the heart, you feel the goodness of your actions in your heart.

Express truth, not opinion

When dealing with our neighbour, in practically every situation, every event, we have an opinion. Opinion is contradictory. When I have an opinion in any situation, either one of us is wrong, or both of us are wrong, and it is usually the second. Many opinions, many wrongs. When we put our neighbour first, opinion ceases. There is therefore a unity between myself and my neighbour.

Opinion is not conversation; conversation is putting facts together. By putting facts together, we will end up agreeing with each other. Why? Because in every event, in every situation, there is only one truth. So from now on we must stop using the words 'In my opinion', and instead use the words 'I am thinking aloud'.

And as for choosing the correct words by putting our neighbour first, when in life does this happen? The answer is this: when you are in the company of an older person or in conversation with an elder family member who you have great respect for. In that moment, you will notice that you become silent until you find the correct words, the correct answer. How did this happen?

Put half your attention on your mind and the other half on your breath, and you will notice that you become silent. Why? Because by now, you are in touch with your conscience and your conscience shows you that your mind is wrong, so you become silent and take your time.

And that is the way to be with yourself, always and everywhere. So from now on, have respect for yourself and choose the correct words, the correct answer, always and everywhere. Love your neighbour as you should love yourself, your real self, your conscience.

Speak in double form

Not answering a question directly is a way of finding the correct words. By not answering directly, but in double form (saying one thing and meaning another intentionally), you help your neighbour also. You make them ponder, *think twice*, get in touch with their conscience and feel the joy in their heart.

By not speaking directly but in double form, nothing from outside can touch us. By not becoming identified with life's events, by not taking our senses seriously, we develop objective reasoning. By not speaking directly, we compel others to think twice and develop their objective reasoning also. By not answering a question directly but in double form, we get in touch with our conscience. Why? Because in order to speak in double form we must think twice. Only by thinking twice can we get in touch with our conscience. Not thinking twice is mechanical.

Many myths and religious texts, including the parables in the gospels, have a twofold purpose: to teach us, firstly, that we are not what our senses show us, and secondly, not to speak directly.

By putting my neighbour first, I don't take myself seriously, as I do now. When we get in touch with our conscience, we stop speaking mechanically, we feel insulated from life's influences, we don't take our senses seriously, and nothing from outside can touch us.

If someone asks me a serious question, I shouldn't always reply directly, but answer either with another question or with a light-hearted joke by speaking in double form. However, if this is not possible at that precise moment, it is better to say nothing.

Not taking our senses seriously is the way to speak in double form, which will put a smile on my neighbour's face. And this can be done when we learn to speak spontaneously from the heart. For example, if my neighbour asks me the question, "How are you? Are you well?", my answer could be "Of course, what else did you expect? You are here, aren't you?"

By putting our neighbour first, we understand others, and that makes us intelligent. When we know we are right, we take criticism with a smile. And by doing so, we make our present good, without error, and above all, without judgement. Put your neighbour first and you will never be wrong.

Many problems and misunderstandings exist because we are not logical. Knowledge is not logic. You have logic when you put the other person first. Knowledge does not belong to me. Understanding? Yes, that is mine.

Consider externally always

All misunderstandings today happen because, from an early age, we teach our children to speak directly by example. Speaking directly comes from the senses alone. We speak and act according to what we see or hear, and so on, without first *considering externally*. Considering externally means putting yourself in the position of others. In doing this, we stop speaking or acting according to the evidence from our senses alone, but rather from the heart. By considering externally we put our neighbour first, and we remember ourselves, and when this method is in action, we are in touch with our conscience in the heart.

Be correct, not just polite

When a child does something wrong to another person, the first thing we do is to ask, 'Did you say sorry?', which is a man-made law. And man-made laws are always mechanical. Teaching our children to say sorry after doing something wrong is the same as telling them that by saying sorry they can do as much wrong as they like. Saying sorry after doing wrong is a form of putting ourselves first. By *feeling* sorry over our intention to do wrong, we put our neighbour first, before ourselves, and we come second. Be polite not for the sake of being polite, but for the sake of being correct.

Neighbour countries

And now, as neighbouring countries or nationalities, let us put the other first and all wars will stop. Are we so selfish so as not to care about each other's existence, let alone that of our children? We start wars and send our children to die in them, under the names of patriotism, religion, etc. I don't understand how anyone can kill, but then again, actually I do – a lack of conscience.

As we have said, by getting in touch with our conscience, we develop our objective reasoning, which is under the Law of Three – the three centres and the three forces of our being act simultaneously together. When one of the three centres and one of the three forces is missing, that makes an animal. In the animal, the Intellectual Centre is lacking and only two forces are present – the positive and the negative, the event, and the reaction. The reconciling force is absent.

A person who is not in touch with his or her conscience lives life as an animal. The positive part of the Emotional Centre and the reconciling force are missing.

That is why we have been destroying each other's existence by the millions. And this has been going on for thousands of years. Could there ever be a worse animal on earth than man?

So, how can our differences be resolved? The solution can be found in the parable of the unjust steward:

> *There was a certain rich man, which had a steward; and the same was accused unto him that he had wasted his goods. And he called him, and said unto him, How is it that I hear this of thee? Give an account of thy stewardship; for thou mayest be no longer a steward. Then the steward said within himself, What shall I do? For my lord taketh away from me the stewardship: I cannot dig; to beg I am ashamed. I am resolved what to do, that, when I am put out of the stewardship, they may receive me into their houses. So he called every one of his lord's debtors unto him, and said unto the first, How much owest thou unto my lord? And he said, A hundred measures of oil. And he said unto him, Take thy bill, and sit down quickly, and write fifty. Then said he to another, And how much owest thou? And he said, A hundred measures of wheat. And he said unto him, Take thy bill, and write fourscore. And the lord commended the unjust steward, because he had done wisely: for the children of this world are in their generation wiser than the children of light. And I say unto you, Make to yourselves friends of the mammon of unrighteousness; that, when ye fail, they may receive you into everlasting habitations. He that is faithful in that which is least is faithful also in much. If therefore ye have not been faithful in the unrighteous mammon, who will commit to your trust the true riches? And if ye have not been*

> *faithful in that which is another man's, who shall give you that which is your own? No servant can serve two masters: for either he will hate the one, and love the other; or else he will hold onto the one, and despise the other. Ye cannot serve God and mammon.*
>
> *(Luke 16:1–13)*

This parable can be understood only if, instead of 'wise', we use and explain the Greek word that was used first – *phronimos*, the understanding of which is essential. *Phronimos* means wise and above all peaceful. And now the steward, by being *phronimos*, by using his objective reasoning, by being intelligent and peaceful, found the solution to the problem. And so it should be with us. Many problems of this world and differences between countries can be resolved in this manner, as in the parable, by giving half of what one side demands and by receiving half from the other side, even sixty/forty if necessary. In this way, we still receive the reward, we develop objective reason. And by developing objective reason, we will see and understand all reality. There will be no more clashes, no more wars. Instead, we will make friends and enjoy a tranquil and peaceful existence in 'everlasting habitations'.

Let us examine the following quotes from the parable:

> *...for the children of this world are in their generation wiser than the children of light.*

We are not born with objective reasoning, but we can learn to reason objectively as the unjust steward did. By reasoning objectively, we (the children of this world) can become wiser than the angels (children of the light).

> *And I say unto you, Make yourselves friends of the mammon of unrighteousness;*

Be just and indulgent to the weaknesses of others.

> *No servant can serve two masters: for either he will hate the one, and love the other or else he will hold onto the one and despise the other.*

No one can serve two masters, the mind which is based on the evidence of the senses, and conscience which is based on what is true and good.

> *Ye cannot serve God and mammon.*

You cannot live according to your conscience and remain as you are, living from your mind alone, which is after earthly treasures (*mammon*) only.

To understand why we should put our neighbour first, I will also explain the following parable:

> *The kingdom of heaven is like unto a net that was cast into the sea, and gathered of every kind which, when it was filled they drew up on the beach, and they sat down, and gathered the good into vessels, but the bad they cast away. So shall it be in the end of the world, the angels shall come forth and sever the wicked from among the righteous, and shall cast them into the furnace of fire.*
> *(Matthew 13:47–50)*

Now, life is like the sea with every 'kind' in there, good and bad, right or wrong, which enters into our mind – the net, as in the parable. And by now since I am in touch with my conscience in the heart, the kingdom of heaven, I 'draw up' what is in my mind, 'sit down' with my conscience and take my time. And since only conscience can perceive what is true and good, I gather and keep the good in my heart, and I cast the bad away.

> *So shall it be in the end of the world, the angels shall come forth and sever the wicked from among the righteous.*

This happens through self-observation. 'The wicked' is when we put ourselves first, through our ego, self-pride, self-interest, self-conceit, vanity and so on. 'The righteous' is when we put our neighbour first. By putting our neighbour first, we get in touch with our conscience, we become impartial and sincere, we develop objective reasoning, which is the aim of our existence.

And then let it be the end of the world. Yes, but which world? The world of today, in which we put ourselves first. So now let us build a new world, a world in which we put our neighbour first.

5

ESOTERIC CHRISTIANITY

By applying the Method, we get in touch with our real selves and find the truths hidden in early Christian and other religious texts. Since I am not a literary man, and have only limited knowledge of other religions, I will connect Christianity with this method and leave it to others from other religions to do the same, since all religions come from the same source.

In the next chapter, I will explain the hidden truths contained in the parables of the New Testament gospels. But first, I will talk about the established Christian ideas which are taken literally today.

Prayer

In the New Testament gospels, Christ often asked his disciples to pray. But what is prayer? Prayer is the same as having attention, with the difference being that we can have attention according to the Method every day, every minute of the day. And that is what Christ meant when he told his disciples many times to pray continually. But of course, praying continually – if taken literally

– is impossible in everyday life; if only we could understand the meaning behind it, which is as we said, to have attention continually.

By praying, we have attention and remember ourselves, but prayer is a kind of medicine; it relieves for a while, but does not cure. After praying, we forget ourselves again and go back to where we were before. There is no more attention. Keep your attention on your breath and you will remember yourself always and everywhere.

Belief in God

When we learn to live according to our conscience, we no longer have a need to *believe* in God; we will *know* God. God is our conscience. So by following the Method and getting in touch with our conscience, we no longer need to search for the way to God. This method, to an atheist or a believer, is the same. It is a way to know oneself, to be linked consciously with all parts of oneself.

Conscience is God's gift. Conscience has been given to us by God to show us His love and become His image.

> *There is more joy in heaven for one man perfected by his*
> *own efforts than in ninety-nine naturally evolved angels.*
> *(C.S. Nott, 'Teachings of Gurdjieff' 1961)*

The kingdom of God (your conscience) is within you, in your heart. Thanks be to God for His unspeakable gift. By living according to our conscience, we will become His sons and daughters. Could there be more joy than that in Heaven?

Repentance and sin

It has been said, unless you repent, you cannot enter into the kingdom of heaven. Repentance in the original Greek is *metanoia*. Metanoia is made up of two words: *meta* (after) and *noia* (mind). Unless you think again, 'after the mind', you cannot enter into the kingdom of heaven. Only by thinking again, after the mind, can I get in touch with my conscience, and by doing so, I see very clearly that what my mind was showing me was wrong. So I 'repent', I change my mind. And since conscience is in the heart, I enter into my heart, into the kingdom of heaven.

Repentance has nothing to do with sin. When we don't know what we are saying or doing, it simply makes us ignorant, not sinners. So from now on accuse no one, as each does the best they can according to the knowledge that they possess. It is not other people's *fault*, only their ignorance. That is why Christ said on the cross:

> *Father forgive them, for they know not what they do.*
> *(Luke 23:34)*

Ignorance is not a sin. When we know what is true and good and yet we don't act according to it, that makes us sinners. But now that will never happen. By living according to our conscience, there will be no sinners in this world. Why? When we know what is true and good, we will *always* act accordingly, because our conscience won't let us do otherwise. When we live according to our conscience, we can never do harm, as in the following saying by St Augustine:

> *'Love God and do as you will'.*

Love your conscience (both God and conscience are based on what is true and good), and then live your life as you will, since you cannot love God *and* do harm. In living according to the Method, there is no retreat from life; in fact, there is the opposite. You will live life to the full by being present and conscious always and everywhere. Being conscious is freedom. When we live according to our conscience, we feel free from external influences.

When we get in touch with our conscience, we see all the bad things around us that affect us. This is quite normal since we have just been born again. Through self-observation, we question experience and learn for ourselves, and by doing so, we don't need any teachers. We become our own teacher, we become two-natured – me and my teacher, the observed and the observer. And by being so, we build our soul. The soul is the highest level of being that we can create in ourselves. The conscience and heart are already there – we need only to get in touch with them.

By observing and questioning ourselves, we see very clearly our own ignorance, and when that happens, we are on the right path. Then we become silent, because by now we are in touch with our conscience, and our conscience does not let us do otherwise.

> *Let every soul be subject unto the higher powers. For there is no power but of God: the powers that be are ordained of God.*
>
> *(Romans 13:1)*

By observing ourselves, we create our soul, which leads us to our conscience. The higher powers are what is true and good – our conscience. Conscience and God are one.

> *Whosoever therefore resisteth the power, resisteth the ordinance of God: and they that resist shall receive to themselves damnation.*
>
> *(Romans 13:2)*

As we have said, conscience and God are one. Whoever resists conscience, resists the 'ordinance' of God. Without conscience present, there is no real life and no peaceful coexistence.

Therefore, we should build a new world, a world whose leaders are elected based on their good deeds, and not on their 'much speaking'; a world based on objective reason, impartiality and sincerity.

The cross

According to the Gospels, Christ died on a cross. Yet the symbolism of the cross has escaped us for centuries. The esoteric meaning becomes clear when we live according to our conscience.

When we do not live according to our conscience and speak in the way we are accustomed to speaking now, we repeat the same old things and speak automatically. When we speak from our heart, through the guidance of our conscience, this stops. There is no more repetition. Everything that comes through our conscience is always spontaneous. Spontaneity is the one thing that makes life more vivid; there is new life at every moment.

Now since every moment is the present, living according to our conscience at every moment makes our present good, since conscience is based on what is true and good. It has been said that what we sow we reap. The future is the result of the present: by seeing our past misdeeds, and working on them at every moment of the present, we make the present good, and the future will be the result of that. And this is the meaning of the cross – the past must be crucified in order to make the present good.

When we make our present good, then our past is pardoned, our past is cured. Why? Because we realise that the past has happened because we didn't know any better, and that means our past is no longer any concern of ours. And it is the same for our future, since the future is the result of the present. The future is no longer any concern of ours because it will become the present at some point. So there is only one way left for us to go – up, above, and reach our prime source. When that happens, the whole process of this method takes place.

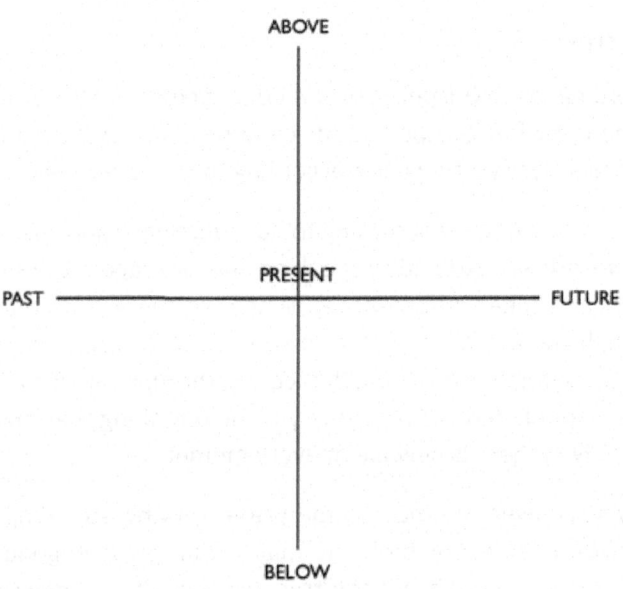

Figure 3: The meaning of the cross.

6

ESOTERIC MEANING OF THE GOSPELS

The aim of the New Testament gospels is to tell us to make contact with the prime source, our essence. To achieve this, we must think twice. And that is the reason why Jesus spoke in parables: to make us think twice. The parables and sayings of Jesus are themselves one of the main pieces of literary evidence for the existence of the kingdom of God. They are all about our conscience and the love of our neighbour, as we will see in what is to follow.

So now, with the Method, the key if you like, let us open all the doors and let light come into our houses, into our hearts.

Parable of the mustard seed

In this parable from the Gospel of Mark, Jesus speaks about the outcome of getting in touch with our conscience:

> *And he said, Whereunto shall we liken the kingdom of God? or with what comparison shall we compare it? It is like a grain of mustard seed, which, when it is sown in the earth, is less than all the seeds that be in the earth. But when it is sown, it groweth up, and becometh greater than all herbs, and shooteth out great branches; so that the fowls of the air may lodge under the shadow of it.*
>
> *(Mark 4:30–32)*

At the beginning of our development, our conscience (the kingdom of God) is like a mustard seed. Its influence over our actions is very small. But when we work on ourselves, there will come a time when it will become greater and act faster than our minds.

The 'fowls of the air' in the parable represent thoughts from above (from our conscience), and not from the mind alone.

Parable of the Growing Seed

Here is a similar allegory from the same Gospel:

> *And he said, So is the kingdom of God, as if a man should cast seed into the ground; And should sleep, and rise night and day, and the seed should spring and grow up, he knoweth not how. For the earth bringeth forth fruit of herself; first the blade, then the ear, after that the full corn in the ear. But when the fruit is brought forth, immediately he putteth in the sickle, because the harvest is come.*
>
> *(Mark 4:26–29)*

The kingdom of God, our conscience, is like a seed; it will grow. But at first we don't know how to live under the guidance of our conscience, since it is new territory for us. Therefore, we must take our time. But when we start living this way, all fruit, all knowledge of truth, will become our property. Conscience acts spontaneously and is in abundance – as the parable says, 'the harvest is come'.

Parable of the Ten Virgins

The following parable is about thinking twice:

> *Then shall the kingdom of heaven be likened unto ten virgins, which took their lamps, and went forth to meet the bridegroom. And five of them were wise, and five were foolish. They that were foolish took their lamps, and took no oil with them: But the wise took oil in their vessels with their lamps. While the bridegroom tarried, they all slumbered and slept. And at midnight there was a cry made, Behold, the bridegroom cometh; go ye out to meet him. Then all those virgins arose, and trimmed their lamps. And the foolish said unto the wise, Give us of your oil; for our lamps are gone out. But the wise answered, saying, Not so; lest there be not enough for us and you: but go ye rather to them that sell, and buy for yourselves. And while they went to buy, the bridegroom came; and they that were ready went in with him to the marriage: and the door was shut. Afterward came also the other virgins, saying, Lord, Lord, open to us. But he answered and said, Verily I say unto you, I know you not. Watch therefore, for ye know neither the day nor the hour wherein the Son of man cometh.*
>
> *(Matthew 25:1–13)*

To explain this parable, first let us make clear the meaning of the lamp and the oil. The lamp represents the mind. But to have light in the mind (to understand), we must reason, we must have oil.

Only by having attention and thinking twice before we act do we develop objective reasoning. And this is what makes us wise. Not thinking twice is mechanical; he who does not think twice does not think well.

Let us look again at a few sentences from the parable:

> *They that were foolish took their lamps, and took no oil with them: But the wise took oil in their vessels with their lamps.*

The foolish did not bring oil with them – they do not think twice before the event in order to reason objectively and understand.

> *And the foolish said unto the wise, Give us of your oil; for our lamps are gone out. But the wise answered, saying, 'Not so'.*

We cannot give our understanding to anyone; we develop understanding through our own efforts – we are our own understanding. And here I will take the opportunity to explain the esoteric meaning of the Commandment, 'thou shalt not commit adultery': you cannot take someone else's understanding. Your understanding is your own.

> *... go ye rather to them that sell, and buy for yourselves. And while they went to buy, the bridegroom came; and they that were ready went in with him to the marriage: and the door was shut... Lord, open to us. But he answered and said, Verily I say unto you, I know you not.*

After buying oil, the 'foolish' came back to the marriage (the union) and found the door shut. Thinking twice after you act is useless, the door is shut. Only by having attention will we be in contact with the Lord, with our conscience, and be ready for any event.

Watch therefore, for ye know neither the day nor the hour wherein the Son of man cometh.

Remember yourself ('watch therefore') every day, every minute of the day, and be ready for any event, or as the parable says 'before the Son of man cometh'. The 'Son of man' is when only the positive and negative forces take part (see Chapter 2), as opposed to the 'Son of God', when all three forces act simultaneously and harmoniously. Only by remembering ourselves can we get in touch with the Lord, with our conscience.

The Good Samaritan

In this well-known parable, we see very clearly how to love our neighbour:

And behold, a certain lawyer stood up, and tempted him saying, Master, what shall I do to inherit eternal life? He said unto him, What is written in the law? How readest thou? And he answering said, Thou shalt love the Lord thy God with all thy heart, and with all thy soul, and with all thy strength, and with all thy mind; and thy neighbour as thyself. And he said unto him, Thou hast answered right: this do, and thou shalt live. But he, willing to justify himself, said unto Jesus, And who is my neighbour? And Jesus answering said, A certain man went down from Jerusalem to Jericho, and fell among thieves, which stripped him of his raiment, and wounded him, and departed, leaving him half dead. And by chance there came down a certain priest that way: and when he saw him, he passed by on the other side. And likewise a Levite, when he was at the place, came and looked on him, and passed by on the other side. But a certain Samaritan, as he journeyed, came where he was: and when he saw him, he had compassion on him, And went to him, and bound up his wounds, pouring in oil and wine, and set him on his own beast, and brought him to an inn, and took care of him. And on the morrow when he departed, he took out two pence, and gave them to the host, and said unto him, Take care of him; and whatsoever thou spendest more, when I come again, I will repay thee. Which now of these three, thinkest thou, was neighbour unto him that fell among the thieves? And he said, He that showed mercy on him. Then said Jesus unto him, Go, and do thou likewise.

(Luke 10:25–37)

In order to have compassion for others, the Emotional Centre must be present first. But in the lawyer, as well as in the priest and Levite, the Emotional Centre was missing. Only the Samaritan acted with compassion towards the wounded Jew (and Jews and Samaritans were not on friendly terms at the time).

The lawyer had all the knowledge necessary ('Thou hast answered right'). But knowledge alone does not make the whole of a person. That is why Jesus told him to 'go and do likewise'. Have compassion for your neighbour. But it is one thing to know, and another thing to do. Only by doing what we know is true do we understand.

The Lord's Prayer

We can use the Method to explain the esoteric meaning of the Lord's prayer, a central prayer in Christianity :

> *Our Father, which art in heaven, hallowed be thy name. Thy kingdom come. Thy will be done, as in heaven, so in earth. Give us day by day our daily bread. And forgive us our sins; for we also forgive everyone that is indebted to us. And lead us not into temptation; but deliver us from Evil.*
>
> *(Luke 11:2–4)*

'Thy kingdom come' refers to the kingdom of God, our conscience in our hearts. By praying (having attention) every day, every minute of the day, we will be in touch with our conscience every day, every minute of the day. God does not interfere but He gave us His replacement, our conscience, and by living according to our conscience, the will of God 'will be done as in heaven, so in earth,' since conscience and God are one.

God, as we said, is under the Law of Three: the affirming, the denying, and the holy reconciling. This is the meaning of 'give us, day by day, our daily bread', which becomes clearer when we reflect on the original words in Greek: *ton arton hemon ton epiousion*. The word *epiousion*, which describes the bread, means 'super-substantial'. And the significance is this: to make bread, we need flour and water – and fire to unite the two.

So it is with us. For anything real to happen, three forces must combine, but we have been given only the positive and negative forces, and that is what makes us a self-developing organism. We have the possibility and the ability to create the third force, the reconciling force, by ourselves, through our own efforts. And this can be done by forgiving everyone that is indebted to us, which in real terms means putting your neighbour first, and expecting nothing in return. In doing so, we bring into ourselves the third force, the reconciling force, and become a unity, 'as it is in Heaven'.

The Beatitudes

Matthew 5:3-12 describes Jesus' famous Sermon on the Mount, which contained what are known as the Beatitudes. In each of the Beatitudes, Christ is speaking of those who have made the effort to work on themselves.

> *Blessed are the poor in spirit: for theirs is the kingdom of heaven.*
>
> *(Matthew 5:3)*

To be blessed means to feel joy. The 'poor in spirit' are those who know that they don't know, those who see their own ignorance. By observing ourselves we will be in touch with our conscience, enter into our hearts and feel joy.

> *Blessed are the peacemakers: for they shall be called sons of God.*
>
> *(Matthew 5:9)*

The peacemakers are those who use the reconciling force to become impartial and sincere. They will be in touch with their conscience and therefore can be called 'sons of God'. Conscience and God are one.

> *Blessed are they which are persecuted for righteousness' sake: for theirs is the kingdom of heaven.*
>
> *(Matthew 5:10)*

This verse refers to people who are mistreated by others for being impartial and sincere. When we are impartial and sincere, we uncover our buried conscience in the heart (the kingdom of heaven) and feel joy, despite the actions of other people towards us.

> *Blessed are ye, when men shall revile you, and persecute you, and shall say all manner of evil against you falsely, for my sake, Rejoice, and be exceeding glad: for great is your reward in heaven.*
>
> *(Matthew 5:11–12)*

When we don't react with anger to the displeasing behaviour of others, for the sake of our conscience, we will enter into our hearts and feel joy.

Woe unto you lawyers!

In this verse, Jesus refers to people whose Emotional Centre is lacking:

> *Woe unto you, lawyers! for ye have taken away the key of knowledge: ye entered not in yourselves, and them that were entering in ye hindered.*
>
> *(Luke 11:52)*

As we have said, in order to reason objectively, we have been given three centres – the Intellectual, Emotional and Moving Centres – to act together and simultaneously and in harmony. When this happens, we get in touch with our conscience in the heart. But in the religious scribes of that time (lawyers), who had the knowledge without understanding, this did not happen.

In today's legal system, this hardly ever takes place either. And I will explain. In a legal case, the court will often base its decision on a judgement that has been given in a similar case. Often, this doesn't fully take into account the individual. As such, the Emotional Centre is missing, because the system does not let those involved enter within, into the heart. Therefore, they are not in contact with their conscience, which is the key, the key of knowledge. Only conscience can perceive what is true and good, not the mind, since conscience is impartial and sincere.

The same predicament applies to the media, where the man-made law that we call free speech is often used to justify language in which the Emotional Centre is missing.

The servant is not greater than his lord

The following passage is about the relationship between mind and conscience:

> *Remember the word that I said unto you, The servant is not greater than his lord.*
>
> *(John 15:20)*

The mind is not greater than the conscience. It is the servant of our conscience. When we are about to speak or act, the mind serves us with knowledge. But only conscience can perceive and choose the good from the bad in order to guide us. The mind cannot comprehend conscience; when used alone, the mind judges according to our likes and dislikes.

Whosoever drinketh the water that I shall give him shall never thirst

Jesus talks about the mind and knowledge again in this verse:

Everyone that drinketh of this water shall thirst again: but whosoever drinketh of the water that I shall give him shall never thirst; but the water that I shall give him shall become in him a well of water springing up into eternal life.
(John 4:13–14)

When we live from the mind alone, we shall 'thirst again' (for the knowledge of truth). We repeat the same thoughts and habits over and over; there is nothing new. With the knowledge of truth applied in practice ('the water that I shall give him'), we will release our conscience ('a well of water springing up into eternal life'). Conscience is spontaneous and in abundance; there is new life at every moment.

Except a man be born of water and the spirit

As we have seen in the previous verse, 'water' was understood to mean the knowledge of truth. And we can see this again in the following verse:

Except a man be born of water and the spirit, he cannot enter into the kingdom of God.

(John 3:5)

The meaning here is that we need the knowledge of truth, and 'the spirit', a higher level of being that we create in us through self-observation, in order to be reborn. Only then will we enter into the kingdom of God, our conscience.

Enter at the straight gate

In the passage below, Jesus speaks about the effort needed to uncover our conscience:

> *Enter ye in at the strait gate: for wide is the gate, and broad is the way, that leadeth to destruction, and many there be which go in thereat: Because strait is the gate, and narrow is the way, which leadeth unto life, and few there be that find it.*
>
> *(Matthew 7:13-14)*

Many things may enter the mind – good and bad, right or wrong. But the mind alone cannot judge, it is mechanical; the mind alone is always wrong. We are not what enters into our minds. We are what comes out from the heart through the guidance of our conscience. Only conscience can perceive and choose between good and bad, right or wrong. Conscience is based on what is true and good. Conscience makes life more vivid, and since a big effort is needed to get in touch with it ('narrow is the way'), there are few who find it.

And straightway his ears were opened

The following verse describes what happens to us when we speak from the heart:

> *And straightway his ears were opened, and the string of his tongue was loosed, and he spake plain. And he charged them that they should tell no man.*
>
> *(Mark 7:35-36)*

When we speak from the heart, our voice has greater resonance, not a greater volume ('And the string of his tongue was loosed'). Our words are essential and precise ('and he spake plain'). The extraordinary person is simple in behaviour. And finally, you cannot give your understanding to anyone ('And he charged them that they should tell no man'). Your understanding is your own.

Why do ye not understand

When we speak from the heart, our tone of voice has a different sound. We can see this in the following verses:

> *Why do ye not understand my speech? Even because ye cannot hear my word.*
>
> *(John 8:43)*

> *He that is of God heareth God's words: ye therefore hear them not, because ye are not of God.*
>
> *(John 8:47)*

Jesus was asking why they didn't understand the tone of his voice that comes from the heart, nor perceive the meaning behind his words. He was speaking in double meaning. When we are in contact with our conscience in the heart, when we are 'of God', we hear and perceive the knowledge of truth and good.

Except ye repent

In the previous chapter, we said that repentance in esoteric Christianity means thinking again. Here is a verse in which Jesus talks about repentance:

> *And those eighteen upon whom the tower of Siloam fell, and slew them, think ye that they were sinners above all men that dwelt on Jerusalem? I tell you Nay: but except ye repent, ye shall all likewise perish.*
>
> *(Luke 13:4-5)*

This event takes place when the disciples reported to Jesus that Pilate had murdered some Galileans. 'Repent', as we explained, is think again through our conscience and 'change our mind'.

The mind is a tool, but when used alone, it is always wrong. So the meaning is: think again, this time through your conscience, the real side of you, and change your mind. This is the way to feel present and alive. When we do not live according to our conscience, we do not live according to what is true and good. This is the same as being non-existent ('we shall all likewise perish'). And that is also the meaning of 'let the dead bury their dead' (Luke 9:60), which Christ says elsewhere.

Let not thy left hand know what thy right hand doeth

The following is another verse about loving our neighbour:

Take heed that ye do not your alms before men, to be seen of them: otherwise ye have no reward of your Father which is in heaven. Therefore when thou doest thine alms, do not sound a trumpet before thee, as the hypocrites do in the synagogues and in the streets, that they may have glory of men. Verily I say unto you, They have their reward.

But when thou doest alms, let not thy left hand know what thy right hand doeth: That thine alms may be in secret: and thy Father which seeth in secret himself shall reward thee openly. And when thou prayest, thou shalt not be as the hypocrites are: for they love to pray standing in the synagogues and in the corners of the streets, that they may be seen of men. Verily I say unto you, They have their reward. But thou, when thou prayest, enter into thy closet and when thou hast shut

thy door, pray to thy Father which is in secret; and thy Father which seeth in secret shall reward thee openly.
(Matthew 6:1-6)

First, let us explain the meaning of the left and right hand. We can understand this turn of phrase if we imagine using the right hand to give something to someone and then the left hand to take.

When we do good, and then go and speak about it out of self-pride, we 'have our reward' – we become a clever person who is at the same time stupid. But by continuously having attention and obverving ourselves, as we have seen in Chapter 4, we will do good and expect nothing in return. When that happens, we enter into our heart ('thy closet'), get in touch with our conscience ('shut thy door') and take our time. When we start living according to our conscience (which acts 'in secret'), we will be 'rewarded openly' (by feeling the joy of our good actions from the heart).

Feed my sheep

Another verse which shows us how to love our neighbour can be found in the Gospel of John:

Jesus saith to Simon Peter, Simon, son of John, lovest thou me more than these? He saith unto him, Yea, Lord, thou knowest that I love thee. He saith unto him, Feed my lambs. He saith unto him again a second time, Simon, son of John, lovest thou me? He saith unto him Yea, Lord, thou knowest that I love thee. He saith unto him, Tend my sheep. He saith unto him the third time, Simon son of John, lovest thou me? Peter was grieved because he said unto him the third time, Lovest thou me? And he said

> *unto him, Lord, thou knowest all things, thou knowest that I love thee. Jesus saith unto him, Feed my sheep.*
>
> *(John 21:15-17)*

Jesus was trying to show Peter what conscious love is. Peter in the gospels is represented as the man with knowledge alone. Knowledge alone divides us all; knowledge alone loves and judges according to our likes and dislikes. Jesus was teaching Peter the second commandment, the 'love of thy neighbour', and asked him whether he loved him more than the others, and Peter said yes.

So Jesus said to Peter, if you love me, 'feed my lambs', 'tend my sheep' and 'feed my sheep'. In other words, if you love me, put your neighbour first. And this is the way to show conscious love. It should make no difference to you who I am, what counts is who you are: be good to everyone, love everyone. However, it is one thing to know, and another thing to do.

Love your enemies

> *Ye have heard that it was said, Thou shalt love thy neighbour, and hate thine enemy. But I say unto you, Love your enemies, and pray for them that persecute you; That ye may be sons of your Father which is in heaven.*
>
> *(Matthew 5:43-45)*

Pray, as we have said, means have attention. Have attention and feel compassion towards others' ignorance ('Love your enemies and pray for them...'), and you will be in touch with your conscience in your heart ('That ye may be sons of your Father which is in heaven').

Forgive men their trespasses

Here is a verse in which Jesus talks about forgiveness:

> *For if ye forgive men their trespasses, your heavenly Father will also forgive you: But if ye forgive not men their trespasses, neither will your Father forgive your trespasses.*
>
> *(Matthew 6:14-15)*

By getting in touch with our conscience in our hearts, we forgive others for their transgressions; forgiveness comes from the heart. When our conscience begins to guide us, we see our ignorance and then the past is forgiven, since it wasn't our fault, but the fault of ignorance. Only conscience can perceive what is true and good. But when we are far from our conscience, we are unable to forgive others and we remain ignorant.

Taste of death

In the following verse, Jesus talks about our false personality, which must be diminished as we have said:

> *Verily I say unto you, That there be some of them that stand here, which shall not taste of death, till they have seen the kingdom of God come with power.*
>
> *(Mark 9:1)*

The 'death' here represents the death of false personality, which must take place if we are to be in touch with our conscience (the kingdom of God).

The eye of a needle

Elsewhere in the gospels, false personality is represented by 'a rich man':

> *Then said Jesus unto his disciples, Verily I say unto you, That a rich man shall hardly enter into the kingdom of heaven. And again I say unto you, It is easier for a camel to go through the eye of a needle, than for a rich man to enter into the kingdom of God.*
>
> *(Matthew 19:23–24)*

The meaning here is a man who is 'rich' (in false personality) has little chance of entering into his heart and getting in touch with his conscience (the kingdom of God).

Give not that which is holy unto the dogs

In the gospels, we can find allegorical examples of what happens when the reconciling force is missing:

> *Give not that which is holy unto the dogs, neither cast ye your pearls before swine, lest they trample them under their feet, and turn again and rend you.*
>
> *(Matthew 7:6)*

As we have said earlier, the dog is an animal in which we can clearly see two opposing forces at play, the event and the reaction. Therefore, 'dogs' refer to those who react blindly. So the meaning is do not give the knowledge of truth to them, as they will contradict you. Nor open your heart before those who will just try to find you at fault with their opinions.

If ye were blind

In the previous chapter, we spoke about the difference between ignorance and sin in esoteric Christianity. The following verse makes this distinction clear:

> *Jesus said unto them, If ye were blind, ye should have no sin: but now ye say, We see; therefore your sin remaineth.*
>
> *(John 9:41)*

The meaning of this is: If you were ignorant, you would have no sin. Ignorance is not a sin. Ignorance can be redeemed in time. But when we do not wish to see our ignorance, we remain sinners.

Unclean spirits

Elsewhere in the gospels, ignorance is represented by 'unclean spirits':

> *And unclean spirits, when they saw him, fell down before him, and cried, saying, Thou art the Son of God. And he straitly charged them that they should not make him known.*
>
> *(Mark 3:11–12)*

When they were given the knowledge of truth, they saw their ignorance. When we get in touch with our conscience, we see our ignorance, and at first we feel remorse ('they fell down before him and cried').

And when we get in touch with our conscience we must become silent ('they should not make him known'), since conscience is a new territory for us, and take our time.

If thy right eye offend thee

In Chapter 3, I described the role of self-observation in the Method. The gospels do not talk directly about self-observation, as the meaning is mostly hidden. However, when we think twice, we can find allegorical verses such as the following from the Gospel of Matthew:

> *And if thy right eye offend thee, pluck it out, and cast it from thee: for it is profitable for thee that one of thy members should perish, and not that thy whole body should be cast into hell. And if thy right hand offend thee, cut it off, and cast it from thee: for it is profitable for thee that one of thy members should perish, and not that thy whole body should be cast into hell.*
> *(Matthew 5:29-30)*

When we observe ourselves sincerely, we may see many shortcomings and weaknesses in us, but do not despair. Work on one defect at a time, since to work on all the defects of the body at the same time is impossible.

Judge not, that ye be not judged

We always see other people's wrongdoings, never our own colossal blunders, as Jesus makes clear in the following verse:

> *Judge not, that ye be not judged. For with what judgment ye judge, ye shall be judged: and with what measure ye mete, it shall be measured to you again. And why beholdest thou the mote that is in thy brother's eye, but considerest not the beam that is in thine own eye? Or how wilt thou say to thy brother, Let me pull out the*

> *mote out of thine eye; and, behold, a beam is in thine own eye? Thou hypocrite, first cast out the beam out of thine own eye; and then shalt thou see clearly to cast out the mote out of thy brother's eye.*
>
> *(Matthew 7:1-5)*

We must first observe ourselves sincerely, see our ignorance, and then change. Then, and only then, can we be impartial towards others.

Note on Bible version used

When I started writing this book, I had in my possession traditional translations of Bible verses, mostly from the King James Bible. And now reading more recent versions, I see very clearly that the traditional translations better reflect the esoteric meaning of the original text. Here are three examples to illustrate what I mean.

> *No one can serve two masters. Either you will hate the one and love the other, or you will be devoted to the one and despise the other. You cannot serve both God and money.*
>
> *(New International Version, Matthew 6:24)*

The older version uses the word 'mammon' instead of money. Mammon comes from the old Greek word *mammonas*, which refers to earthly treasures. The mind alone, out of self-interest, seeks earthly treasures such as power, possessions and pleasures, rather than just money. We can compare this explanation to the story of Hercules (see page 70–72).

> *Why is my language not clear to you? Because you are unable to hear what I say.*
>
> *(New International Version, John 8:43)*

In the older version, Jesus asks 'why do ye not understand my speech?' (see page 57). The word 'speech' is a translation of the old Greek word *lalia*, which refers mainly to tone of voice. The modern version uses the word 'language', which refers only to words.

> *You have heard that it was said to the people long ago,*
> *'You shall not murder, and anyone who murders will be*
> *subject to judgment.'*
> *(New International Version, Matthew 5:21)*

'Murder' refers to killing a person, but older versions have: 'thou shall not kill'. Kill has to do with not just a person, and that is where the double meaning occurs: kill in our heart, for example through vanity (see page 3), which is very difficult to redress.

7

MYTHS, LEGENDS AND MESSENGERS

As I have said, many myths and legends are about what we need to do to develop and get in touch with our conscience. I will now connect the Method with the limited knowledge in my possession of myths, legends and other allegorical accounts within and outside Christianity. I will attempt to explain them without any wiseacring, and taking nothing literally, so that they will be understood very clearly by everyone.

Moses

In the Old Testament, there is the story attributed to Moses of the movement of the children of Israel away from the power of the Pharaoh and Egypt, in another direction, through the wilderness, and eventually reaching the Promised Land.

The Pharaoh here represents the evidence of the senses which rules us, and Egypt the literal and sense-based truth. In order for us to get in touch with our conscience, we must escape from the evidence of the senses and the literal and sense-based truth. When we get in touch with our conscience, since conscience is new territory to us, it is the same as the wilderness. But by continuing to live according to our conscience and reaching our essence, the Promised Land, we will eventually see all the benefits that we will receive. All knowledge of truth and good from the foundation of the world will become our property.

Signs of Buddhahood

In the Buddhist tradition, among the signs of Buddhahood, it is written:

- Shoulders and arms are beautifully moulded.
- His arms are long, so that when he stands without bending his hands can touch his knees.
- A well-formed head and forehead.
- Forehead is broad and straight.
- His voice is like that of Maha-Brahma.
- His tongue is soft and long.

As for the shoulders and arms, this is the practical outcome of the Method, which relaxes the muscles, causing the shoulders to drop and the wrists to loosen. And as for the head and forehead, when the muscles are relaxed, there is no more tension in the face.

When all that happens, we gain attention. Our mind turns to our breath and we remember ourselves, our real selves, and enter into our hearts.

Then we speak from the heart. When we speak from the heart, through our breath, our voice is like that of Maha-Brahma, it has greater resonance, not a greater volume (*his tongue is soft and long*).

When all that happens, the whole aim of the Buddhist religion will be at hand, and then follows the rebirth: Nirvana.

Nirvana (conscience) is a complete liberation from Samsara (false personality). False personality, as we said, comes under the influence of ego, self-conceit, self-pride, self-esteem, self-interest, self-justifying and vanity.

Nirvana is freedom. Nirvana is devoid of ego, self-conceit, self-pride, self-esteem, self-interest, self-justifying and vanity.

When we live according to Nirvana, Samsara will be diminished. And that is the ultimate goal of the Buddhist religion: what to do to diminish Samsara.

It is said in the New Testament, 'Man does not live by bread alone'. We need the knowledge of truth *and* to put it into practice. By doing so, we get in touch with our conscience. By living according to the Method in everyday life, at every moment, we will be in touch with our conscience at every moment. Then and only then do we feel fed; then and only then do we feel alive.

Atlantis

The Greek philosopher Plato gives an account of Atlantis, an ancient island kingdom that submerged into the Atlantic Ocean. Atlantis, the meaning of which is conscience, was buried in the depths of the waters; and so conscience is buried in the depths of knowledge alone. When we take everything literally, our only reality is the evidence from our senses. And that is what prevents us from living according to our conscience.

Pandora's Box

In Greek mythology, there is the story of Pandora's Box. After her marriage, Pandora received a sealed box as a present from Zeus (God). The box contained an inscription to keep her promise not to open it. But Pandora, out of curiosity, opened the box, and from inside came all of mankind's vices. But at the last moment, Pandora thought again and shut the box, and inside remained Hope, mankind's only blessing.

When we live by the evidence from our senses, curiosity appears, the kind of curiosity that comes from the mind alone. All of our vices that prevent us from living from our real side – conscience – are because we use the mind alone, and the mind alone is always wrong. But there is Hope. By making the necessary effort, we have the possibility and ability, even at the last moment, to think again, and in doing so, get in touch with our conscience in the heart. There is a covenant between conscience and heart; conscience perceives, then the heart will do what is promised.

Hercules

According to another Greek myth, when Hercules reached maturity, he wandered out, sat on a stone, and started thinking about how he should live his life.

Then a rich woman came and said to him, 'Why are you thinking? You are strong; go and get all the gold.'

Then another woman came along, beautiful, and asked him the same thing. 'Why are you thinking? Work, be sincere, do not live

Figure 4: Marble statue of Hercules sitting on a rock.

with the burden of others; good possessions are obtained with hard work. If you are not hungry, you don't enjoy your food; if you don't get tired, you cannot relax; if you do injustice, your soul will not rest.' The first woman was Malice *(Kakia)*, and the second Virtue *(Arete)*.

Later in life, King Euristheas sent him to kill the lion of Nemea and skin it. He also killed the Lernaian Hydra, the great serpent, and won many more battles.

Let me explain: When Hercules reached maturity, he went out and, as represented in ancient artwork, sat on a stone – stones, as we have seen, symbolised knowledge. Hercules had all the knowledge necessary and started thinking what he should do, how he should live his life. But in order to know what is correct, what is good, first we must know what is bad. Devil is also necessary.

So the first woman came along – Malice – the devil as in the parables, wealthy and rich, rich in false personality (i.e. ego, self-interest and so on). Hercules was thinking whether he should use all his powers, all his knowledge, for self-pride, self-interest, and get all the riches and pleasure out there in life.

Then Hercules started thinking deeply, and sincerity appeared, Virtue, and he got in touch with his conscience (sincerity comes from conscience). He said to himself: Why am I thinking about earthly treasures? And then he saw very clearly all the beautiful things he would receive by living according to his conscience.

So by being sincere, Hercules got in touch with his conscience and found God; conscience and God are one – both are based on what is true and good. So now he started living according to his conscience, and because his conscience wouldn't let him do otherwise, he went and killed the lion of Nemea and Lernaian Hydra – all self-interest and self-pride must be killed – and won many more battles. All vices that prevent us from living according to our conscience must be killed.

Helen of Troy

There is also the Greek myth of the Trojan War to free Helen, the daughter of Zeus (God), who was abducted. Helen's beauty and the actions it inspires in the story can be likened to our conscience and the 'war' against false personality. When we stop living from our real side, our conscience, then false personality grows, which as we have said is under the influence of ego, self-conceit, self-pride, self-esteem, self-interest, self-justifying and vanity. In order to free our conscience, which is currently as if in prison, the positive, negative and reconciling forces must be combined together. And for this to happen, a big effort is needed, a big war against all the defects of the body that prevent us from living according to our conscience.

We see this again in the story of St George, who killed the big dragon, false personality.

Figure 5: The myth of St George and the dragon (false personality).

Depications of Cleopatra

A young lady Solange Claustres, who was in contact with Gurdjieff, said in her book[2] that in his flat in Paris she saw a painting of Cleopatra holding an asp towards her heart, the implication being that if her city were to be conquered, she would rather kill herself. And at that moment Gurdjieff said, "She changed the face of the world."

---

2 S. Claustres, *Becoming Conscious with Gurdjieff* (Eureka Editions 2005), p.54

I would like to take this picture as an analogy. If her city, if her body, was to be conquered, conquered by false personality, she would rather kill herself. The self in this analogy represents the self of false personality, which must be killed in order to free conscience, which is why the serpent is held towards her heart, conscience in the heart.

The serpent here represents the transformation of a being with the knowledge of truth, which gives strength and wisdom. And we can compare this to what Jesus said, "The kingdom of God is within you. Seek therefore to know yourselves, and you shall know that you are in the city and that you are the city."[3]

The kingdom of God, your conscience, is within you (in your heart). Seek therefore to know yourself and you will know that your conscience is within you and that you are your conscience.

---

[3] Taken from the non-canonical Oxyrhynchus Sayings of Jesus, found in Egypt in 1897–1903.

8

MY STORY

Now, to explain the direct manner in which this book is written, it started with events in London from thirty-three years ago. However, it is clear to me now that my life had been introduced in such a way that I would end up where I am today. I say 'introduced', because looking back on my early years I see that I grew up without any adult influences.

When I was about nine years old, my father had a car accident in the Greek city of Thessaloniki, where we were living at the time. It took six months for him to recover, but the taxi driver he used to come home that evening did not make it.

My father was a meat merchant. As a result of the accident, he was unable to continue with his business, which finally led to his decision to take the whole family back to the nearby village where I was born, and I had to stay on my own in Thessaloniki for a few more years to finish my schooling.

At the age of eighteen, I received an invitation from an aunt of mine, Sonia Gurdjieff, in Paris, to join her there and continue my education at university. I accepted. However, because of my type and financial situation, I did not complete my studies.

After three years, I went back to Greece to do my military service for two years, and at the age of twenty-five I visited another aunt of mine, Luba, in London. Luba was pleased to see and get to know me and asked if I spoke English. Since the answer was no, she invited me to stay and learn. This was of course something I had been wishing and hoping for. My aunt had a bistro, 'Luba's Bistro', in Yeoman's Row in Knightsbridge, where I helped her for three months while going to school to learn English. Once again, I gave it all up. Instead, I decided to make my life in London my way. I say my way, but again, looking back, I see that everything was pre-arranged.

One late evening in 1965, I found myself in a smoke-filled casino in London's Bayswater area. There, I met some Greeks from Cyprus playing the poker game. With only fifty pounds in my possession and not much experience, I started playing with those professionals. I began the game with two sevens, a weak hand compared to the others who had two aces, two kings, two pairs and so on. The game involved seven players, each betting 50 pounds. Since there were only 4 cards remaining, the dealer had to apply the rule of the game where the top card goes for everyone. He turned over the card, and it was a seven. With a three of a kind, suddenly the highest-ranking hand in that game, I won 350 pounds. This was a good sum of money at the time, especially to me. As I stood up to take all my winnings home, I was approached by one of those Cypriot Greeks, a tall slender man in his mid-thirties. He asked if I wanted to help him run a poker table in a small nearby casino. I agreed. When I arrived home that night, I saw my wife sleeping in bed. Then my emotions began to take over. I put my hand in my pocket, took out the money I had won earlier and threw it all over her. And the following day, without any experience whatsoever, and with little financial backing, I entered the casino business.

Three years went by and a new law required all small casinos in London to close. What a blessing for me, as it meant I could have new experiences in life. Over the next twenty years, with the help of some more lucky breaks, I went on to run a restaurant, a fashion retail business selling leather garments and cowboy boots, which were popular back then, as well as several retail units selling records, cassettes and CDs. By now I had a family of three children that I valued very much, and a house with a large garden.

However, dealing with all these businesses on my own wasn't easy. In absence of the reconciling force back then, and with an overpowering Emotional Centre, my reactions to external events were affecting my physical and emotional wellbeing. With painful sores constantly developing on my head, my health was in serious decline. At the same time, my inability to cope with the pressures of business and raising a family put an enormous strain on my relationship with my wife, an angel in disguise.

So in the summer of 1983, I decided to rest for a few days. I remembered that in London I'd met someone who said he owned a club on a Greek island, so I decided to go there.

At the establishment belonging to this acquaintance of mine, there was a young man behind the bar who asked me to send him a book upon my return to London. I agreed. He came and gave me a folded piece of paper with the title of the book he wanted. I opened it and there I read: *Teachings of Gurdjieff*.

When I read the title, I was shocked. How was it possible, so far away from my surroundings, that someone there had asked me to send him *Teachings of Gurdjieff*? I was stunned, but not as stunned as this young man was when I told him that George Gurdjieff was my great-uncle (a term we use in Greek to describe a brother or cousin of a grandparent). My grandfather and George Ivanovich Gurdjieff were the sons of two brothers, Vasilis and Ivan (John) Gurdjieff.

I returned to London and the next day went and bought the book to send to him, like I'd promised. That evening, with all my problems left and right, and my health getting worse, I went home and decided to read a little.

Me in London, circa 1970.

Until then I had never read even one line of my great-uncle's work. The only things I knew were some stories I'd heard in my youth, from my grandfather, Alexander Gurdjieff, later translated to Kiourtzidis when the family moved to Greece.

The following day, I went and bought another copy and sent it to my new friend on the Greek island. I kept the one I had bought in the first place and carried on reading it.

As I read the book, my attention was drawn to the fact that I had to work on just one thing: *To bear the displeasing manifestations*

My grandfather and I around 1956.

of others. When I read this, I immediately realised where I had gone wrong in my life. I saw very clearly that the reason for my state was my life conditions and that my Emotional Centre was too dominant. My ever-present conscience wouldn't let me do wrong, but at the same time I didn't know how to handle life's events which were opposed to my nature and being. But knowing what is wrong is not enough. I had to find a way to bring down my Emotional Centre. My aim was to do what was needed for my development and that's when I discovered a method: doing physical work to relax the muscles and free the body.

I will describe what I did as follows. With a long-handled garden hoe, I would chop up a patch of soil in my garden in a steady, rhythmic manner, starting from the bottom of the patch and working from one side to the other. When the entire patch of soil had been completed, I would dig the same patch in the same manner, working from the top side to the bottom. I would do this from one to several hours at a time.

The physical work that I did to relax the muscles and regulate the breathing.

This physical activity, traditionally used for weeding and cultivating soil, was done for no material gain. It was a conscious and voluntary labour that relaxed the muscles, especially the facial muscles, lowered the shoulders, loosened the wrists and regulated the breathing. Moreover, it was a means of gaining attention and feeling permanently present.

By doing this I could see my Emotional Centre coming down. That took a long time, but I neither wanted to nor could give up, as was my type and being.

By now I knew what was true and good: when all three centres in a person work together and simultaneously, with none stronger than the other, that is how to deal with adversity in life. And that took twelve years.

At that time, I felt the need to write down everything I had to remember to do to work on myself, for me. And I say for me, but now I see very clearly that it wasn't just for me. As I said earlier, everything in my life was pre-arranged, and I took the decision to put it out in the open in this book, to be seen by everyone without shame. And I do so in order to make it easier for others, so that it will be possible for us to see ourselves, only by ourselves, and without any shame, since we are created as self-developing organisms.

And now I would like to add the outcome of my efforts of twelve years. One day, walking in the garden, I saw my wife at the window, looking at me with a slight smile on her face; I went inside and said to her, '*mous*, is there a husband in this world who loves his wife more than I do?' And she answered and said, 'No'.

9

THE OBSERVED AND THE OBSERVER

Along my own path of self-development, which began 33 years ago, I regularly made notes to myself. These reminded me to use events in life as an opportunity to work on myself ('the Work'). This chapter is based on these old papers, which I have presented as some final words of guidance to the reader undertaking this path. They will apply to anybody, since human nature is the same.

Consider internally never

Establish as a principle not to pay attention to other people's opinions. You must be free from people around you, and when you are free inside you will be free of them.

When with people, always remember yourself, and think of what you are saying, doing, even the way you move. Your conscience does not allow you to hide from yourself. God does not interfere but He did give you His replacement: your conscience.

Do not see anyone you do not wish to see or do anything out of kindness that you would not otherwise do. Be polite not for the sake of being polite but for the sake of being correct.

When you finish a conversation, good or bad, never ruminate; remove it from your mind immediately, so that you feel present and remember yourself.

Take nothing seriously. But if anyone says to you, "Oh, because you don't care," your answer should be, "No, because I do care". I don't take things seriously because I am serious. Taking things seriously is discordant; by not taking things seriously, not for your sake but for your neighbour's, you put your neighbour first. Put your neighbour first from the smallest event to the highest (especially the smallest). Small things make life. Without connecting yourself with your neighbour, there is no life.

The close people around you can save you, by taking them as they are without expecting them to change. By doing so you get paid back, you gain force. There's so much good material for the Work if you don't take them seriously, if you do so without expecting them to change. Remember they are God's gift to you, so never reject it; turn a curse into a blessing.

When people say things that are disagreeable, do not make judgements against them. Do not answer with yes or no; if not cunningly with a question to the question, it is sometimes better to say nothing.

Forget about what everybody else is doing or saying; they are not your problem. God has His reasons. We are a self-developing organism, each one must develop him or herself. Not by force but by self-will. You are only responsible to yourself. You need change no one, only yourself.

When you are with people, anyone, think only about the Work. Do only for the Work. If you ever get upset with other people, it is always your fault. The more difficult they are, the more you handle them with a smile. Be against no one.

You cannot bring about negative emotion intentionally, only through ignorance. When there is unpleasantness around you, whether in family or in life, do not be filled with despondency. But consider yourself lucky, welcome it; to handle the situation correctly, passively, is your only medicine. It is food, it is force for you, it is your only way to happiness, it is your everything. So take your time, use the situation and turn it into a blessing. There is a way. The reason you don't do it yet is because you are lazy about acting properly. Consider externally always, be passive and calm. Do not be lazy to make the effort to act or answer correctly.

By bearing other people's 'displeasing manifestations', you enter into the kingdom of heaven as a reward from God. Thank anyone who gives you the opportunity. Even when you drive just say "I" to your breathing. Welcome any opportunity to do the Work – bearing people, traffic, etc. It is much easier to bear things person to person, moment to moment, because you remember yourself and feel present.

You don't have to like. Not disliking is enough. Stop disliking, and then you will like that which you dislike now, because you can, because that is what you will and can do. And because you can do it, you feel great, you love it, and you love them. Love people regardless of their behaviour towards you, it's a great feeling.

You want something very much and somebody prevents you: accept it, leave it for a time, nothing is more important than this Work. Work on yourself, work in connection with others, and you will get what you want later.

Problems and unpleasant events

When something unforeseen happens, try to handle it on the spot, no matter how bad it looks. It is the thinking after that you must stop. Cut it off. The thinking after is the worst part. Cut it off, make yourself completely empty. Do not take it in. You must do that, it is your cure.

When a thought comes into your mind that you shouldn't dwell on, don't. Otherwise you become identified with it. Thinking is like a motion picture, one thought follows another, which left unchecked, can lead to unpleasant things. In other words, you get identified with your thoughts. Thinking is taking in. Dwelling is taking in. Despondency is considering inside. Consider externally always, internally never. Always move freely.

The idea is not to avoid unpleasant events, the idea is not to identify with them. It is a hundred times better to meet an unpleasant situation with non-identifying, than to meet a hundred pleasant situations. For that, do not reject unpleasant situations, just meet them with non-identifying.

Never complain, do each thing at a time, be free. Complaining is negative. Dealing with each situation in the moment, consciously, gives force. If you have no situation to deal with, you gain nothing, so welcome it for the Work.

With the help of the Work, you can do anything. You need nothing, you can deal with anything, you can sort anything out. You are you. So anything that happens, any problem – it is not a problem any longer. With the help of the Work you can say yes, you can say no, or you can say nothing. You know how.

Never try to sort out a problem with your mind; you get identified with it and then it is difficult to cope. In fact, there is no problem if you don't think about it.

Take it like a game. As soon as your mind goes somewhere you don't like, take your mind off it: non-identifying. And be pleased that you can do it, because behind non-identifying there is the Real "I".

You cannot change your life, but you can change yourself, your attitude to life, by non-identifying. It makes no difference whether it's in work or anything else. What you must do is stop identifying immediately.

You cannot remember everything at once, just remember yourself and then you remember everything. You don't have to think how your life is going, only about freeing yourself inside. Sort nothing out as there is nothing to sort out; take life as it comes, and act accordingly.

You don't free yourself inside by not having problems, but by separating yourself from your problems – it makes no difference how many problems you have.

Any problem, even the worst kind, you should not try to explain; take it only as material for the Work. And only when it happens, not before, not after, only when you are there. There is nothing to solve. Acknowledge the problem and take it off your mind, even your dreams. Just live the present. Look, don't dream.

Stop thinking out of time and place. You say stop your thinking; why? Because by thinking you are building up a situation, and then a problem. In placing your attention on what has happened, it becomes the same as a real problem. So say to yourself, 'If I don't think about a problem, there is no problem'. That is why you should stop your thinking.

It is a good thing – when you start to identify with a thought or a situation – to turn your mind and attention immediately to something else, something of a completely different order. For example, when you go to bed and an unpleasant thought comes to mind that prevents you from sleeping, stop it immediately, and you can do that by putting your mind into something else entirely. And that happens because the mind can take in only one thing at a time. It is all down to you what you put in there.

Never try to sort out a past situation by dwelling on it because, if you do, you are living it again. You can sort nothing out by ruminating; concentrating on the present is one hundred times better.

Try to remember this: life's unpleasant events should never touch you inside. Remember to remember to make this your God.

Tasks and effort

There are two very important things you must change in yourself. First: you must change your attitude towards doing. Think of 'what'; 'how' is for when you get there. Second: take your time, use your breathing, your sensing, for whatever you are doing.

Observe yourself in anything that you do; watch how you do it. Are you taking your time? Are you doing it slowly? Are you doing it with self-remembering? Are you keeping your attention on your breath? Do you finish one thing before you start another? Are you doing it calmly? Are you sensing yourself? Remember to remember yourself – that prevents you identifying with whatever you do.

Always remember to do things slowly; you can do this by having half of your attention on your breathing and the other half on whatever you are doing or saying. Remember to remember yourself and be passive; have attention on your breath and then, and only then, speak or act.

When you have two or three things to do, no matter how small, do one, stop, then do another; because this is life, take your time. If you don't take your time, you are tense. You get identified with what you are doing.

No one thing is more important than another. Writing consciously is as important as building a house consciously or lighting a cigarette consciously. Blessed is he or she who is doing it.

Never get involved in too many things. Do things only that are agreeable to you and look after yourself – the right way, of course.

When you get up in the morning do not think what you have got to do; take your time. You owe nothing to anyone. Just engage in self-sensing. Never think or talk about how you are going to do one thing or another; think not, say not. You need only peace, everything else can wait.

Stop placing too much importance on details, on unimportant things. Put your mind only to what is important to you. And each time you have something to do, do not do it for that something. Instead, look forward to it for the Work.

You must always remember to make an effort; effort is always necessary. Effort to do things slowly, to walk slowly, effort not to ruminate after an event, effort to remember yourself. Zest with ease.

Even when you feel good you must not forget the act of self-remembering. No internal talk.

Faith and belief

Faith is something you don't need proof of. Leave yourself to God. He Knows. Think about nothing else and let fear go. Put yourself into His hands. He is fearless.

Whatever you do from now on, just do, don't think about a finish. What you had to clear up, you have cleared up. Take things as they come, day by day. Never think of tomorrow, let it be. If wrong, if somebody wrongs you, it does not hurt you more than thinking of tomorrow, so let it be; have Faith.

Do not think of tomorrow. Your Father in Heaven is going to look after you, as He did before, so He will do again. Enough effort is needed to make the present good, and when you realise that, then He will leave you alone; when you leave the rest to Him, when you have faith in Him, when you stop thinking of tomorrow. Now, only now, is you.

You will suffer until you get there, until you become perfect. So much to be stripped of. So be patient, there are many more battles to be won.

Do not expect definite results, just enjoy yourself along the way, not only the results. Do not expect everything to go smoothly. How can you know everything if you don't go through the worst? He is with you for good ends, but you must go through the worst.

No matter how much you suffer, God is the only one who can save you. No matter what happens, you must put your mind on Him. Cast away fear.

Earning a living

From now on, earn your living not just for the money but also for the Work. Use temptation for inner development outside of time and place. Go on, refuse temptation and use everything as a means, not an end.

You need to earn a living; you cannot eliminate that completely. But if your work or business arrangements are not as you wished, it doesn't matter. These are non-entities. You have millions within. Just grasp that. Give up all non-entities, and go after the real thing: your cure.

If something is going badly at work, cut it off and throw it away. Do not cover yourself in despondency, just wait. It is completely up to you. If something's gone bad, cut it off and cast it away, but wait until and only if that happens. Everything must become like a play – take nothing seriously. As soon as a bad thought comes to mind that you don't wish to dwell on, don't, even for a second. Turn your attention elsewhere. Always remember that.

Never put your thoughts too much into your career or business, good or bad, but on the Work always. Forget earthly treasures; just accept what you are given and go after real gold: the gold is within you.

Mistakes and remorse

If you make a mistake now, use it as material for the Work and stop thinking about it. Never think about what will happen later. By thinking and dwelling on the past or future, you lose attention, and then mistakes follow.

If you make a so-called mistake, it is not a mistake. It is His answer to your question. So do not bury yourself in despondency. Be pleased with His answer, so that you can do the Work correctly. Do not be negative – accept and try again. Whatever you have said and done is said and done. No need to dwell. Just say I to your breathing.

When you make a mistake, and find the reason, you don't feel bad because you found it. Thank the person for giving you the opportunity to be sincere with yourself and develop your objective reason.

Remember, you are learning. If you make a mistake, it doesn't matter. You are only a young child, a new child; it is bound to happen. But be strong, there are more days to come. Just think that one day there will be no mistakes.

Taking things seriously

You can do what you want if you take your time and don't immerse yourself in despondency. There is nothing serious: what matters is how you react. Be passive, take your time and do not take things seriously; deal with them with a smile. You must do all of that. You are committed anyway. Nothing is important, only your God.

The Present

Today, think about what you must do today. Tomorrow, think about what you must do tomorrow. Getting up in the morning, think not of yesterday or tomorrow. Thinking of today, the now, is conscious, and, like anything conscious, it gives force.

The present is time. Time is breath. The present is breath. When you realise that, and you live only for now, then He will leave you alone. He only wants you to enjoy your life now, can you find a better way than His?

Are you so blind as not to see that life is now? Wait! Tomorrow is going to be now, and the now never hurts you, only the tomorrow. Tomorrow, later or before is negative; anything not present is negative. Thoughts are not present, so are negative.

Bad talk, bad associations, bad feelings of forgetfulness. Good talk, good associations – these things are always forgotten. The only thing that you never forget – that can never be forgotten – is the present.

The present is always with you, wherever you go, whatever you do. The present is there whether you are getting out of bed, getting dressed, before going out, after going out, meeting people, etc. The present is everything; it is your lifelong companion, your other self that you should always remember. The present gives you force; love it with all your heart. You must change your way of talking. When you talk, you must sense yourself at the same time. Even when you eat, have attention and savour your food. This is the same as self-remembering. May God guide you always.

I am He, and if I am He, I need not bother about my suffering. And if I am He, I can cure my suffering, I can become He. I am He and if I am He, I need not bother with anything that causes my suffering. I know I am He, that I want to be He, that I love He, that I did it all before, and I can do it now. I am He and if I am He, I shouldn't bother about my suffering, because He wouldn't, and because He is mine, because He is I.

Live only for The Work

Someone owes you money, don't give a penny for it.

Someone offends you, don't give a penny for it.

Life's conditions are against you, don't give a penny for it.

Give everything you have to The Work.

Live only for The Work.